How to Care for Your Budgerigar

CONTENTS

Preface 4

Structure 6

Buying 8

Behaviour.......................... 12

Cages 13

Exercise 20

Aviary................................ 21

Handling 24

Cleaning............................ 25

Nutrition 29

First Aid 33

Bibliography...................... 34

We would like to thank the following for permission to photograph their stock:
Holly Whatley, Pete Neville

Photos b

D1341143

The budgerigar,is one of the best known parrots and the most popular pet bird in the world. Taxonomically it is known as *Melopsittacus undulatus*.

The budgerigar is popular around the world for a number of reasons, such as its cheerful disposition, hardy nature, and ease of feeding and keeping. This publication will help you to keep your pet budgie healthy.

Two cock birds together, a sky blue (left) and a green (right).

Wild Budgerigars

Wild budgerigars are nomadic birds that live in large flocks in the semi-arid parts of Australia. Their diet consists of ripe and half-ripe seeds (particularly millet), green feed and small insects, when available. Wild budgerigars are somewhat smaller than those bred in captivity.

The Australian spring and early summer (October-December) is the usual breeding time, when an abundance of fresh feed and water is available. Small tree holes are used as nests. Brooding is done by the hen. During this time she is fed by the cock, who has no access to the clutch until after hatching.

Temperatures in continental Australia vary a great deal. However budgerigars kept as pets in outdoor aviaries need insulated, draught-free sleeping quartersf.

Healthy birds in good condition will breed well and give you much pleasure.

STRUCTURE

The structure and function of birds and mammals are similar, but there are some differences that are important for understanding the keeping, feeding and disease prevention of budgerigars.

Feathers And Skin

Avian skin is very thin; it lacks sweat glands and sebaceous glands and is covered by feathers, which are changed through the process of moulting. Young budgerigars first moult at about the age of three months, depending on the season of hatching. Young budgerigars hatched in autumn may be considerably delayed in moulting. Moulting usually occurs once a year; it may take several months and is often induced by changes in the environmental temperature. The tail feathers are usually shed in spring and autumn.

Respiratory System

Apart from the usual sinuses, trachea, bronchi and lungs (as in mammalian species), birds have air-sacs. These are thin sac-like protrusions from the lungs into the chest and abdominal cavity. They can play an important role during the course of respiratory diseases.

Digestive System

The avian digestive system consists of an oral cavity, oesophagus and crop, proventriculus, gizzard, and a relatively short intestine. Birds do not have teeth. Budgerigars dehusk larger seeds before they swallow them. The dehusked seeds are ground in the muscular gizzard, which is typical for herbivorous birds. This grinding action is assisted by sand and small stones (grit), which the birds swallow when they have access to them.

Reproductive System

The reproductive system of female birds consists of ovaries and an oviduct. The testicles of male birds are inside the abdominal cavity and cannot be seen or felt from outside. Male budgerigars do not have a penis. Copulation is achieved by the male and female pressing their cloacas together.

A normal grey dominant pied cock bird.

BUYING

Pet birds are usually purchased from a reputable pet shop. Before you even enter the vendor's premises, have a good look at the environmental conditions. The place should be clean, tidy and draught-free.

Healthy Birds

Judging the health of an animal requires experience and a bit of good luck. Let the vendor handle the bird, even if you are an experienced bird handler yourself. Handling is a severe stress to untamed birds, which have been known to die from acute heart failure before or after handling.

Before getting close to the bird, stand back and observe it. Healthy birds are alert, hop from perch to perch and show natural shyness. Lack of shyness is often a sign of illness, not of tameness. Healthy budgerigars breathe quietly and fairly rapidly with their beaks closed. An open beak and respiratory noises, watery or creamy discharge from the eyes and cere (waxy skin at the top of

Left: Eggs hatch every other day. The big chick is a week old and one egg is still to hatch.

the beak) are signs of a respiratory problem. The bird must be able to close its beak and dehusk seeds.

The plumage should be smooth and shiny, without feathering defects, except during moulting. Spiky head feathers and a fluffed plumage (to conserve heat) are signs of illness. The vent feathers should be clean and dry; dirty vent feathers are usually an indication of intestinal or kidney diseases. The droppings of a normal and healthy budgerigar are green, harden quickly and have a white 'cap', which is the material excreted by the kidneys.

Reject any bird with fluffed-up plumage, eye or nose discharge, feather defects, crusty skin, dirty vent, overgrown or open beak, missing toes or laboured breathing. Also reject healthy-looking birds which have contact with sick ones.

Single Bird, Pair Or Mixed Group?

If possible, keep a pair or a mixed group rather than a single bird, as it means more enjoyment for both the birds and the owner. In their natural habitat wild budgerigars live in large flocks, and so mixing sexes is usually no problem, except occasionally during breeding. However, a group of birds will spend more time with each other than with the bird keeper and are likely to become less tame than a single bird.

A single bird is best when a close relationship is to be established with just one person who can give it lots of attention. Single birds have no other living contact, so they need a great deal of human attention and a lot of toys to amuse and stimulate them. Budgerigars left alone for long periods of time may become depressed and start to peck out their own feathers from boredom. This 'vice' is very difficult to stop once the bird has discovered that it can amuse itself in this way.

Male Or Female?

This question is not important in single birds because both sexes make good pets, but if you want a breeding pair, it is important to learn how to sex adult budgerigars. Healthy cocks have a blue or violet cere, hens have a brown cere. Telling the sex of a young bird

The yellow faced blue recessive peacock is feeding the hen with regurgitated seeds.

is much more difficult as fledglings of both sexes have purplish ceres.

Before their first moult, young budgerigars are easily recognised. At the age of six weeks they are fully feathered and have dark horizontal stripes on the top of their head and, except in yellows and whites, a dark tip to the beak. Telling the age of older birds is much more difficult. The bird might wear a closed ring giving the date of hatching. If not, rough but not infected skin on the legs shows that the bird is older.

Colour Mutations

Breeding budgerigars is very rewarding for the enthusiastic aviculturist because they abound in colour mutations. There are four colour series based on two ground colours. The green and yellow colour series are based on a yellow ground colour, the blue and white colour on a white ground colour. These four colours occur in light, medium and dark shades, and three additional colour factors complicate the picture. The Budgerigar Society recognises over 100 standard colour varieties.

Some of the common colour varieties are the light green, dark green, olive green, sky blue, cobalt, mauve, light yellow, dark yellow and olive yellow. Other varieties include the red-eyed albinos and lutinos, the recessive and dominant pieds, opalines (with a V-shaped colour area between the wings), cinnamons, grey, white and yellow wings, lacewings, spangles, crested and tufted budgerigars.

These colour mutants are very attractive, but their character is no different from that of standard ground colour budgies. So there is no need to be choosy about colour if you just want a cheerful pet bird.

To transport your budgie, use either a transport box with holes or wire netting on only one side or a small transport cage covered by a cloth, which should prevent draughts. An untamed budgerigar should not be transported in a large cage as it might panic and hurt itself.

Quarantine

Bird keepers who already own other birds are well advised to keep any newcoming bird separate and under observation (quarantined), until they can be reasonably sure that it is healthy.

Apart from the risk of transmissible diseases, new birds may have problems adjusting to their new environment. They may be bullied by other birds or may turn out to be rowdies themselves. It may be helpful to place the newcomer in a small transport or show cage within the aviary for a few days until it is accepted by the bird community.

Mixing With Other Avian Species

In Australia wild budgerigars live in large flocks, so that living together with many similar species is part of their natural behaviour. Budgerigars mix well with many other small parrots, like cockatiels, but they may bully canaries.

Mixing With Other Pets

Budgerigars may be kept with trained docile dogs but not with cats. However, dogs and budgies should not be left alone together. If you have a cat in the house, your budgerigar should be permanently caged in a large flight cage, and the cat should have no access to the room where the cage is kept.

The minimum cage size for a single budgerigar should be 60cm long, 50cm high, and 40cm deep, so that the bird can spread its wings without touching the cage wire. The cage for a pair should be longer, at least 70cm long. Many budgie cages do not reach these minimum dimensions, which is unfortunate because small cages restrict the bird's exercise, leading to obesity.

A pair of blue recessive pieds - the hen is on the right and the cock is on the left.

At least two sides of the cage wire should be arranged horizontally for climbing, and it should be narrow enough to prevent birds from getting their heads stuck between the wire. Some breeders and veterinarians dislike round cages which they feel confuse the bird's orientation. Round cages also tend to be too small to permit sufficient exercise.

Your local pet shop owner will be able to show you a selection of cages and explain the differences between the various designs and materials so that you can see which is best for your use.

Sand, Grit, Grills

Budgies like to spend some of their time on the ground where they search for grit, small stones and sand that help the muscular stomach (gizzard) grind the dehusked seeds. Metal grills prevent the bird getting to the bottom of the cage. They are intended to keep the birds separated from their own droppings, but their disadvantages outweigh their advantages. If the recommended cleaning routine is followed, the risk of catching a disease from the droppings is quite minimal.

Gravel paper, ie, paper with sand or seeds glued onto it, may help to keep the bird's toe nails trimmed but it does not satisfy its desire to pick and scratch in the sand on the floor. Although gravel paper helps keep claws short it is very abrasive and can damage the bottom of your budgie's feet. It is better to use sand on the base of the cage and a gravel perch cover over just one perch in the cage.

Perches

Cages are usually sold with wooden or plastic perches of a standard diameter. It is better to replace these with natural branches of varying sizes, about 0.5-2.0cm. This forces the bird to constantly alter its toe muscles when hopping from perch to perch. The branches can be from various fruit trees and should be free of bird droppings. You should wash the branches before placing them in the cage.

Apart from the toe exercise, natural branches have other

benefits. Budgerigars chew the bark, which contains vitamins and other nutrients, which also keeps them amused. Once the natural branches are chewed clean (normally after 1-3 months), they should be replaced with new ones.

Perches should not obstruct the narrow space within the cage. If two perches are at least 40cm apart, with no obstacle between them, the budgerigar will have to use its wings to jump from perch to perch. Leave a distance of 10cm between perch and wire so that

A variety of toys are available for the amusement of birds (and bird keepers): swings, bells, balls, mirrors, ladders and so on. As long as they do not restrict the bird's movements and consist of unbreakable material, they are useful, particularly for single, lonely birds.

15

the budgie's tail feathers do not rub against the wire as it turns. Do not place feed or water containers below perches, so they are not contaminated by droppings.

Cage Fittings

Other cage fittings include drinkers, feed containers, waterbowls, cuttlefish bones and toys. Toys are important for single budgerigars that are often alone, but do not fill the cage with toys to the point where the bird cannot move around freely.

A common type of drinker consists of a plastic bottle with a metal spout for drinking. The bottle clips to the cage side and the system relies on gravity. The spout must be of durable material to resist the budgie's chewing power and should be cleaned regularly to remove algae which grow on the inside of the drinker. Other types of water and feed containers are open cups made of heavy plastic, earthenware or porcelain. It is best not to put water or food on the floor where it might be soiled by droppings.

The drinking water should be changed at least twice daily because bacteria such as coli and staphylococci multiply rapidly, particularly under warm conditions. Contaminated water can lead to severe and often lethal crop and gut infections and some birds might refuse to drink altogether, leading to dehydration.

Most budgerigars like to have a bath at least every other day, although some seem to dislike water. Baths are either transparent bath houses (a dark bath might scare the bird) or shallow tip-proof saucers placed on the floor. The water must be tepid and must be changed daily. Remove bath saucers after the daily bath to prevent the cage getting wetter. Only use antiparasitic bath additives if ectoparasites (mites) are actually diagnosed because many birds drink from the water in which they bathe.

Budgerigars dehusk seeds before swallowing the kernel, leaving a lot of empty husks lying around. Blow the empty husks from the top of the seed containers to make sure that enough feed is left.

Right: A light green cock bird fluffs up his feathers when he is displaying to the hen during a courtship ritual.

Fresh or green feed, sprouted feed, fruit and vegetables should be offered in a separate container or clipped to the cage wire.

Cuttlefish bone belongs in every cage. It is usually clipped to the cage wire. The bird uses it for beak trimming and as a source of calcium and phosphorous.

A variety of toys are available for the amusement of birds (and bird keepers): swings, bells, balls, mirrors, ladders and so on. As long as they do not restrict the bird's movements and consist of unbreakable material, they are useful, particularly for single, lonely birds. Do not overload the interior of the cage with them.

Nestbox hygiene is the key to the survival and future development of the nestlings. Nestboxes should be disposable or easy to clean. Disposable cardboard boxes have definite hygienic advantages but are cumbersome to make and can be destroyed easily. Non-disposable nestboxes, made of chipboard, solid timber or plywood, must be cleaned and disinfected before each new

Cuttlefish bone belongs in every cage. It is usually clipped to the cage wire. The bird uses it for beak trimming and as a source of calcium and phosphorous.

clutch. Brooding temperatures and humidity inside the nestbox favour the growth of fungi, which can cause fatal respiratory infections. Large cracks, extra ventilation holes and open inspection flaps may be responsible for draughts and chilling of the nestlings. Nesting material should consist of highly absorbent sawdust or fine woodshavings.

Location

The cage's location is very important for the bird's physical and mental health. Any bird, particularly the single bird, needs contact with the family. Therefore, the cage should be at approximately the same height as a human head (because this is the part of a human that a budgerigar is most familiar with) and should be in a light, draught-free location. The cage must not be positioned in direct sunlight.

The kitchen is too damp and too dangerous for flying exercise, halls are too draughty, and bedrooms usually too quiet. Also, the bird should not be carried around from room to room. Therefore the most logical place for a cage is often the family room, where the TV set is located in many households. TV light does not harm your budgerigar, but the bird should be several metres away from the set and outside the direct line between remote control and television.

Lighting And Temperature

As mentioned above, the cage should be located in a well-lit spot that also offers shade. The normal light in a family home is sufficient. Your bird will be more settled if you cover the cage at night. The cover should cut out the light, but let in fresh air. It should not make the cage hot and stuffy during the night.

Budgerigars are relatively hardy birds. Under their native conditions in Australia they sometimes even experience light frosts. Nevertheless, extreme temperature fluctuations should be avoided and excessive heat often does more harm than good. Temperatures between 17 to 24°C (62 to 75°F), depending on the relative humidity, should be comfortable for budgerigars.

EXERCISE

Many cages are too small to allow a budgerigar sufficient flying exercise, therefore budgerigars should be allowed regular flying exercise in a room.

Before allowing a new bird out of the cage for flying exercise you must be confident that the bird is sufficiently tame and that all danger spots have been removed. Other pets, particularly cats, dogs and larger parrots should be out of the room. Windows, glass doors and mirrors should be screened or the curtains drawn so your bird does not fly into them. Other common danger spots are jugs and jars containing fluids such as milk or juice, vases, open aquariums, open fireplaces, heaters, stoves, candles, spiny plants and objects, open gaps and drawers.   Budgerigars will spend most of their time on certain perches. The area underneath such perches should be protected so that droppings are easily removed and the uric acid does not damage the furniture or carpets.

The bird should never be fed outside the cage. If it knows that feed is only available inside the cage, it will usually return to the cage in due time without you having to go through the process of chasing and catching it. The cage door should always be open and there should be a perch in front of it to make it easier to get inside. If the bird has to be caught, use a cloth or a fine mesh, not your naked hand. Tame birds will perch on a finger and are thus easily carried into the cage.

A budgerigar exercising its wings

Your budgerigars can be kept in outdoor aviaries, as long as certain conditions are met. Principally, outdoor aviaries should be draught-free and dry; they should face the sun and include a shaded, insulated shelter room. Avoid proximity to industrial smoke, busy and noisy traffic, pigeon lofts, other aviaries and poultry farms. Vermin and moist conditions are prevented by a sloping concrete floor and narrow guage wire mesh but for cost reasons this type of construction is often rejected. Pea shingle which can be hosed down at regular intervals, or coarse sand which can be raked clean are both suitable alternatives to concrete and more ornamental.

A typical outdoor aviary containing a variety of budgerigars. It should give enough space for exercise, have a roof for shelter and be made safe from vermin.

Rodents can be kept out by burying the mesh down to a depth of 30cm. The mesh around the bottom of the aviary should be fine or an overlaying double layer can be used.

The two layers should stop vermin, cat paws and wild birds from getting in, and prevent small birds from getting their heads stuck. Plastic coating on wire mesh is likely to be chewed off. Galvanized wire of the correct gauge (normally 19G) should be used. Cracks and crevices in wooden stakes offer red mites an excellent hiding and breeding environment. Painting with nontoxic paint at regular intervals should destroy such breeding grounds.

Outdoor aviaries should be partly covered by a roof, so that droppings from wild birds, which might contain pathogenic bacteria or parasites, are kept out as much as possible.

Covering only half the aviary roof allows the birds to bathe in light showers, but make sure access to shelter is always available in case of heavy rain. Feed and water containers should always be placed in the covered section. Under cold climatic conditions the drinking water could freeze and may be a problem. Change the water frequently, use containers with heating elements or place drinkers in the shelter room.

Indoor Aviaries

Indoor aviaries are regarded as large cages with sufficient space for exercise. They should be in a light, draught-free location. If you have the space this is the ideal way to house your pet budgies.

Antics

The skills of budgerigars, if allowed to develop to their full potential, are similar to those of cockatiels. They are excellent and enduring fliers, they love aerobatics, and they can mimic simple words and tunes, although not nearly to the same perfection as some of the larger parrots and mynahs. Young male birds are reputed to be more talented with speech than females. The bird must be very young (from six weeks onwards). Start with simple words (its own name, 'hello', etc.). Do not proceed until the first words are repeated

The beautiful colouring of a dominant sky blue pied cock.

correctly. With patient training your budgie will even learn simple tricks, such as lying on its back, spreading its wings or pulling a wagon.

Taming

Budgerigars are relatively easy to tame while still young and kept singly. Taming pairs and older birds is more difficult. Patience is one of the pre-requisites for success. Some authors recommend wing-clipping before taming, although this is not always necessary with budgies. Wing-clipping just makes taming easier.

HANDLING

Some examinations and procedures require you to hold the bird firmly. You should take it into your hand regularly, and a healthy bird should not take offense, as long as it can breathe freely. However, the situation is different with obese birds. Obese birds not used to being handled regularly may die of sudden heart failure due to stress.

Unlike larger parrots or cockatiels, budgerigars can nip but not bite you. Nevertheless, you may wish to put on a light glove. Do not use heavy-duty gloves because you may have problems controlling your pressure on the bird. When trying to handle a budgie, close the windows, draw the curtains, dim the lights but do not switch them off. Use a fine mesh bird net to catch the bird. Try to talk to the bird in a quiet, calming voice and refrain from sudden, sharp movements.

The best way of holding a budgerigar is to close the palm of your hand over the bird's back and wings, while holding the head firmly between your thumb, index and middle fingers.

A budgie will learn to sit on your hand and become very tame if it is trained from a baby.

Cage and cage furnishings must be kept clean, particularly in cages and aviaries with a large number of birds, where the disease risk is greater than in cages with only one or two birds. Hygienic conditions can reduce but not eliminate the risk of infectious disease. Infectious agents can reach your birds via the feed, water, air, or by contact. Vermin such as rats, mice, flies, cockroaches and wild birds may be disease carriers without showing signs of illness themselves. Unhygienic conditions will cause stress to your birds and leave them open to infection.

Cleanliness And Tidiness

Without cleanliness, tidiness, clean air and smooth water-repellent surfaces, hygiene is impossible. Modern cages made of wire and plastic are obviously easier to clean than bamboo or wooden cages. Tidying and cleaning up before disinfection is by far more important than the disinfection itself because disinfectants cannot fulfill their function if the disease agents are protected by dirt and organic matter.

The character of this Lutino hen bird is no different from a normal ground colour budgerigar.

A young budgerigar with the purple cere which makes accurate
sexing more difficult.

Five Steps To Hygienic Conditions

1. Tidy up the cage and remove grossly visible dirt, using vacuum cleaner (in an aviary), shovel, scraper, wire brush and so on.

2. Soak the cage in water (containing detergent or other mild cleaning agent) for up to one day.

3. Clean with hard brush, scraper, wire brush, water, or use steam cleaning equipment in outdoor aviaries. Steam cleans well but does not sterilize because it cools too fast.

4. Dry the cage thoroughly. Without drying, the water left from the previous steps will dilute the concentration of the disinfectants to be employed.

5. Disinfect with one of the many disinfectants available in pet shops.

Disinfectants

Many cleaning agents and disinfectants are available from chemists and pet shops. They are effective against common bacteria, viruses and fungi, but rarely against parasite eggs.

Prevention of ectoparasites (mites) requires an understanding of the biology of these parasites. The single most important ectoparasites of budgerigars are knemidokoptic mites (scaly face or scaly leg mites). They live permanently in or on the skin of their hosts and require special medical care. Treatment for other mites involves spraying the aviary and birds with insecticides, which must be handled with caution because they are highly toxic to man and bird alike.

Cleaning Routine

Daily: Change feed, remove perishable fruit and vegetables. Change drinking water at least twice daily, after cleaning the water containers. Change bathing water and clean bath. Check nestboxes

Millet is a great treat but it is also quite fattening.

of breeders without disturbing birds. Remove droppings, large particles and wet patches from the floor.

Weekly: Tidy up and clean aviary and furnishings with water and brush. Cages should be thoroughly cleaned.

Monthly: Clean and disinfect feed and water troughs, also any toys and plastic perches.

Quarterly-to-semiannually: Change natural perches.

Without water life cannot exist on earth. Water is the single most important part of the diet. It is a grave error to believe that budgerigars, as natural inhabitants of semi-arid zones, do not depend on good quality water.

Drinking water should be clean, free of chlorine, disinfectants and chemical additives. Leave strongly chlorinated tap water to stand for a few hours in a large bowl to permit the chlorine gas to escape. Boiling the water kills germs but makes the water rather tasteless. Do not use poor quality water or water with a high salt content. Nongaseous, bottled mineral water is an expensive but safe alternative. Change the drinking water twice daily to prevent the build-up of pathogenic bacteria, mainly coli bacteria which can lead to fatal crop and intestinal tract infections. Use detergents sparingly.

Budgerigars need mixed seeds as a basic diet. Pet shops usually sell the basic seeds or seed mixtures which contain mostly canary seed, millet, linseed, niger, rape, sometimes oat, wheat or an artificial grain. Artificial grain may consist of flour, dried egg yolk, dried milk, alfalfa meal, iodine, vitamins, and so on. Budgerigars also enjoy sunflower seeds and a selection of seeding grasses, which can be dried during the seeding season. Seed mixtures are usually iodized to prevent goitre, a swelling of the thyroid glands due to iodine deficiency. You can attach iodine blocks to the inside of the cage if you are unsure whether your seed mixture is iodized. Spray millet is a real treat but do not give it every day because it is very rich in energy.

Supplement the above mentioned basic seed diet with a variety of fruit and green food such as apple, carrot, chickweed, dandelion, chickory, spinach and seeding grasses. It is important to wash all green foods, and collect only where you know it is safe and free from insecticides, weed killer, pollution from roads, or any other harmful substances.

Sprouted seeds can partially replace green food, particularly in winter time. Their preparation is quite simple: from your usual seed mixture soak enough seeds in water to make a day's supply; keep in a warm place for 24 hours; rinse thoroughly several times and

This budgerigar's bright, shiny eye shows that it is in good health.

leave standing in a warm place for another 24 to 48 hours. Good fresh seeds should have sprouted by then. Rinse the food to wash off microscopic fungi, and discard mouldy sprouts as they may cause enteritis.

During the brooding and rearing period, breeders like to offer various breeding mixtures, soaked wheat bread, boiled eggs, grated cheese, titbits, and so on. However, do not leave such food for more than a few hours, depending both on the food and the environmental conditions. Breeders also give vitamin preparations during brooding and rearing. There are no scientific objections to this, although a well-balanced diet should suffice, but it is a good idea to supplement the diet with vitamins when your bird is going through a stressful period such as breeding or moulting.

Never give junk food, strongly salted or spiced food, butter, crackers, chips, biscuits, soft drinks and alcohol to budgerigars, much as they might beg for it.

You must protect feed and water from contamination by droppings, and most commercial feed containers are protected by a hood. For the same reasons, you should clip feed containers to the cage wire and should not place them on the floor, unless you have fledglings. Babies may have trouble finding the feed container, and a seed bowl on the floor could help them. Perches must not be fitted directly above feed or water containers. Check feed containers daily, blow away empty husks from the tops, change feed daily and remove perishable fruit and green food.

Feed Storage And Quality

Feed is perishable by nature, which involves fermentation, fungi, bacteria and parasites. Light, high temperature and humidity, lack of ventilation and other factors accelerate feed spoilage. Spoiled and mouldy food will lead to diarrhoea, liver damage, even vitamin deficiencies and death. Feed spoilage can be slowed down by observing the following storage conditions:

Cool: 10-12°C (50-53°F), but not refrigerated, thus reducing condensation.
Dry: Below 70% relative humidity and well ventilated. Tightly closed containers are not advisable.
Dark: To reduce the detrimental effect of light on vitamins and fats.

Vermin-proof: Keep out rodents, beetles, mites and flies which use up the feed and might carry disease agents.
Short: Do not buy in bulk unless you have excellent storage facilities.

The aforementioned storage conditions apply to the storage of seeds. Supplemental feed, such as sprouted feed, fruit, green feed, cheese or boiled eggs, must be given fresh and removed at the end of the day. Never leave such foodstuff in the cage, as it quickly goes mouldy and could also attract flies.

A normal sky blue dominant pied cock looks suspiciously at the camera.

Sick budgerigars lose weight rapidly and must be treated without delay. Inexpert treatment by the owner usually wastes valuable time. If your budgie suddenly becomes inactive this is usually the first sign of sickness. Check with your pet dealer or go to the vet as quickly as you can.

Sick birds are often in a state of shock. Offer your budgie glucose water; feed it but handle it as little as possible, otherwise it might die in your or the veterinary surgeon's hand.

Transport the budgie in a small, warm box with air holes. Do not use a large cage for transport as the frightened bird might flutter around and get hurt. Do take the bird cage along to the vet who then can evaluate keeping and feeding conditions.

Cover open wounds with gauze or tissue paper, but do not treat them with iodine or other antiseptics unless advised by the vet. Talk to the bird in a soothing voice whenever you see or handle it.

Sick birds should be kept warm, possibly close to infrared light. The bird must be able to move away if it feels too hot. Heated 'hospital' cages are commercially available. For very sick birds, pad the bottom of the cage, supply water and feed and fit a low perch.

Although secure, the uniformity of these perches will not exercise the toe muscles as well as natural branches would.

BIBLIOGRAPHY

**THE PROFESSIONAL'S BOOK
OF BUDGERIGARS**
by Maja Muller-Bierl
TS-138
ISBN 0-86622-076-3
This comprehensive and beautiful book provides all the information necessary for the proper feeding, care and breeding of these popular pet birds. Lavishly illustrated, it will be of help to the beginner fancier and advanced aviculturist alike.
Hardcover, 220mm x 285 mm,
144 pages, full colour photographs throughout.

THE PROPER CARE OF BUDGIES
by Dennis Kelsey-Wood
TW-104
ISBN 0-86622-192-1
Written by an acknowledged expert in bird care, and fully illustrated with colour photographs, this is a practical, down-to-earth guide to everything you need to know about looking after budgerigars.
Hardcover, 220mm x 180mm,
250 pages, full colour photographs throughout.

BUDGIES ...getting started
by Evelyn Miller
TT-002
ISBN 0-86622-416-5
With full colour photographs throughout its 100 pages, this book contains all the information needed for the novice budgerigar owner to keep and breed these delightful birds successfully, and will also be of interest and value to the more experienced aviculturist. *Budgies as a Hobby* is a book in the Save-Our-Planet series and all the publisher's profits go to conservation.
Softcover, 175mm x 250mm, 100 pages, full colour photographs throughout.

Bird keeping for the Young at Heart -
by John Early
GB-014
ISBN 1-85279-027-X
Catering for the young, not-so-young, novice and experienced hobbyist, the author presents essential birdcare facts in a highly readable form with a few chuckles thrown in for good measure.
Hardcover, 175 mm x 260 mm,
64 pages illustrated in full colour.

The Budgerigar Society
Membership Department
Spring Gardens
Northampton NN1 1DR

Tel: 01604 624549
Fax: 01604 627108
Website: www.budgerigarsociety.com